Explore Space!

Rockets

by Gregory L. Vogt

Consultant:
James Gerard
Aerospace Education Specialist
NASA Aerospace Education Services Program

Bridgestone Books
an imprint of Capstone Press
Mankato, Minnesota

Bridgestone Books are published by Capstone Press,
1710 Roe Crest Drive, North Mankato, Minnesota 56003.
www.capstonepress.com

062014   008214R

Library of Congress Cataloging-in-Publication Data
Vogt, Gregory.
    Rockets/by Gregory L. Vogt.
    p. cm.—(Explore space!)
    Includes bibliographical references and index.
    Summary: Describes different types of rockets, how they work, and what they
carry, including delta rockets, Saturn V, and the space shuttle.
    ISBN-13: 978-0-7368-0198-0 (hardcover)
    ISBN-10: 0-7368-0198-7 (hardcover)
    ISBN-13: 978-0-7368-9168-4 (softcover pbk.)
    ISBN-10: 0-7368-9168-4 (softcover pbk.)
    1. Rockets (Aeronautics)—Juvenile literature. [1. Rockets (Aeronautics) 2. Outer
space—Exploration.] I. Title. II. Series: Vogt, Gregory. Explore Space!
TL782.5.V59 1999
629.47′5—DC21
                                                                                    98-45663
                                                                                          CIP
                                                                                          AC

Editorial Credits
Rebecca Glaser, editor; Steve Christensen, cover designer and illustrator; Kimberly
    Danger, photo researcher

Photo Credits
NASA, cover, 4, 6, 6 (inset), 8, 12, 14, 14 (inset) 16, 16 (inset), 18, 20
Photri-Microstock, 10

Table of Contents

Rockets

Rockets are tube-shaped vehicles
that have pointed tops. Rockets have
powerful engines that push them into
the air. Some rockets have fins to help
them travel straight. Space rockets
carry people or satellites into space.

satellite

a machine that circles Earth; satellites take
pictures or send signals to Earth and
receive signals from Earth.

Voyager I

Payloads

Large rockets carry payloads into space. The payload is carried inside the top of the rocket. Satellites and spacecraft are common payloads. This rocket carried the Voyager I spacecraft as its payload. Voyager I took pictures of Jupiter and Saturn.

spacecraft
a vehicle that travels through space; some spacecraft travel to other planets.

payload

fuel

fins

nozzle

solid-fuel rocket

UNITED·STATES

Solid-Fuel Rockets

Rockets burn fuel for power. Rockets use two types of fuel. Solid-fuel rockets burn hard, dry fuel. Flames shoot out the nozzle when the fuel burns. This action creates thrust to lift the rocket into the air.

thrust
the force produced by a rocket engine

payload

liquid
fuel

pump

engine

fins

nozzle

liquid-fuel rocket

Liquid-Fuel Rockets

Liquid-fuel rockets have tanks that hold liquid fuel. Pumps move the fuel to the engine. The engine burns the liquid fuel. Flames shoot out of the nozzle at the bottom of the rocket. This action gives the rocket thrust to leave Earth.

liquid
something that flows freely like water; liquid fuel powers some rockets.

rocket
boosters

Delta Rocket

Delta rockets are medium-sized rockets. They carry satellites into space. Small rocket boosters around a Delta rocket give the rocket extra thrust. This Delta rocket carried a satellite for Canada.

rocket booster

a solid-fuel rocket that is attached to a larger rocket to give extra thrust

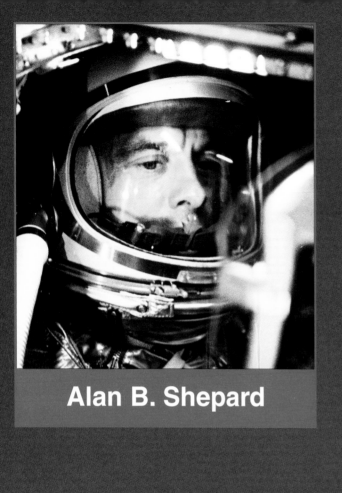

Alan B. Shepard

Man in Space

A rocket took the first American astronaut into space. Alan B. Shepard traveled in a spacecraft carried by a Mercury Redstone rocket. The rocket carried the spacecraft 116 miles (187 kilometers) above Earth.

astronaut
someone trained to fly into space in a spacecraft

capsule

stage 3

stage 2

stage 1

moon lander

Saturn V Rocket

This Saturn V rocket carried a capsule and lander to the Moon in 1969. Three astronauts rode in the capsule. The rocket had three parts called stages. Each stage had engines and fuel. Each stage fell off when it ran out of fuel.

capsule
a small spacecraft in which astronauts ride

17

solid rocket boosters

Space Shuttles

Today, astronauts ride in space shuttles. Solid rocket boosters help lift shuttles into space. The solid rocket boosters drop off when they run out of fuel. The boosters drop into the ocean. Workers refill them to use again.

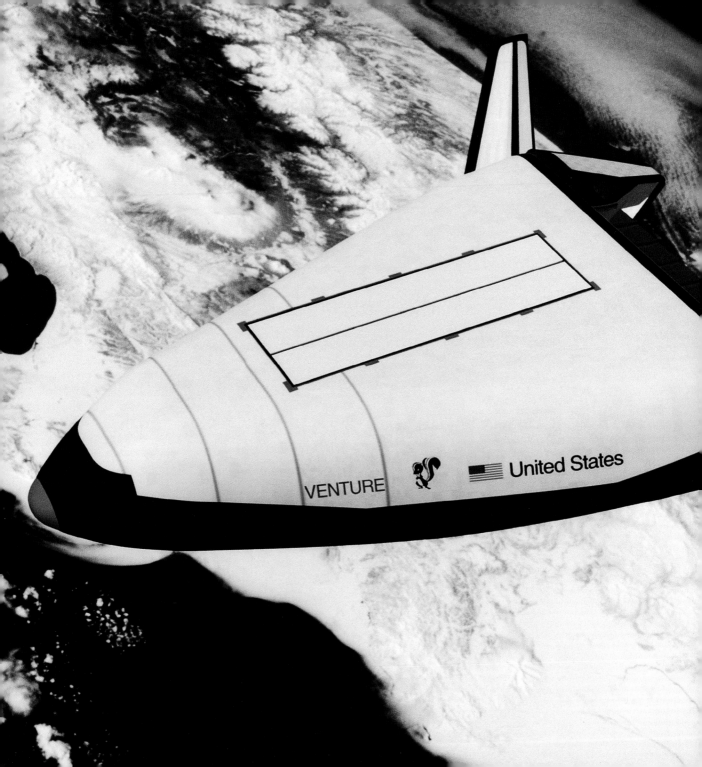

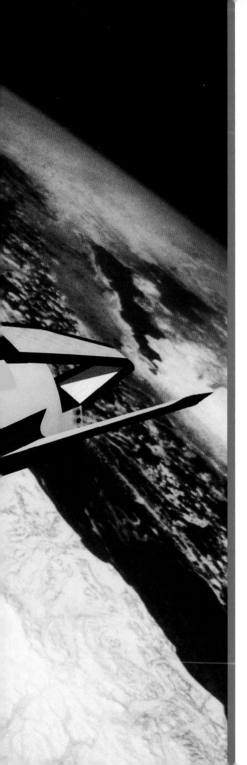

Future Rockets

Rockets in the future may work differently. Scientists plan to build a rocket like this one. People will ride into space inside the rocket. No parts of the rocket will fall back to Earth. The rocket will glide back to Earth like an airplane. People will fly in the rocket again.

Hands On: Launch a Model Rocket

What You Need
2 sheets of construction paper
Tape
Empty 35 mm film can and lid
Scissors
Water
Effervescent antacid tablet

What You Do
1. Roll 1 sheet of construction paper into a tube. This is the body of the rocket. Tape the film can in the tube. The film can must stick out from the bottom of the tube.
2. Cut 4 square pieces from the second sheet of paper. Tape these pieces to the bottom part of the tube for fins.
3. Roll a paper cone for the top of the rocket. Tape it to the tube.
4. Remove the film can lid. Hold the rocket upside down. Fill the can 1/4 full with water.
5. Drop 1/2 of the tablet in the can. Snap on the lid.
6. Set the rocket down right side up. Stand back. The lid will pop off and the rocket will launch.

Words to Know

astronaut (ASS-truh-nawt)—someone trained to fly into space in a spacecraft

engine (EN-juhn)—a machine in which fuel burns to provide power

nozzle (NOZ-uhl)—the small hole in the bottom of a rocket where flames shoot out

pump (PUHMP)—a machine that pushes liquid fuel into a rocket engine

satellite (SAT-uh-lite)—a machine that circles Earth; satellites take pictures or send signals to Earth and receive signals from Earth.

stage (STAYJ)—part of a rocket that holds fuel and engines; a rocket stage drops off when it is out of fuel.

Read More

Miller, Ron. *The History of Rockets.* A Venture Book. New York: Franklin Watts, 1999.

Mitton, Tony, and Ant Parker. *Roaring Rockets.* New York: Kingfisher, 1997.

Snedden, Robert. *Rockets and Spacecraft.* 20th Century Inventions. Austin, Texas: Raintree Steck-Vaughn, 1998.

Internet Sites

FactHound offers a safe, fun way to find Internet sites related to this book. All of the sites on FactHound have been researched by our staff.

Here's all you do:

Visit *www.facthound.com*

FactHound will fetch the best sites for you!

Index